*Mer
The
whic*

*Ivan
Christmas 2021*

# A Reporter's Memoir:

# When the Mob
# Ruled Newport

## By Dan Pinger

ISBN: 978-0-9980991-5-6

First Edition

# Acknowledgments

No question, the most deserving of my heartfelt tribute are the savvy and sensitive top veteran Enquirer editors, Hal Metzger and Jack Ramey. When I was swimming around in search of answers, they threw me a line. I also wish to acknowledge for their friendship and counsel Luke Feck, Maggie (Margaret) Josten, Jack McDonald, Jerry White, Bill Kagler and Ollie James.

This book would never have made it through production if it were not for the talented and smart Ellen DePodesta, my daughter and my publisher. Assisting along the way providing valuable advice was my former wife, Debra Pinger. I wish to thank my sister, Marilyn Glasgow, who has been providing me with valuable counsel since I first began to talk and walk. And then there are the loves of my life:, my daughters Judy Pinger, Karen Winkler, Cory Keller and my sons Dan Junior and Alex Keller, all of whom hold important places in my heart.

# Table of Contents

# Chapter 1

## Assignment: Newport

In 1958, I was a young general assignment news reporter on the staff of the *Cincinnati Enquirer*, the largest and most prestigious news gathering organization within hundreds of miles. I had been a reporter for two years, after spending 13 months as a copy boy, which was then the only path to a staff position.

Working with me as a copy boy was a fellow who had just earned his Ph.D. in English, and another with a master's degree in political science. All of us were kept busy with tasks major and minor, running here and there with stories to be published or do whatever else, including running out to a restaurant to get cups of coffee for staff members. The reporters were college graduates, but none were from journalism schools. Preferred were those with liberal arts degrees, the maxim being that "the Enquirer will teach them journalism." Only the most deeply committed survived.

Prior to being a copy boy, I was at Duke University Law School and became disinterested in becoming a lawyer. The news bug bit me at Rollins College, where I was on the school newspaper's staff for three years, the final one as editor-in-chief. I enjoyed cutting through the hearsay to write what was really going on (and was once expelled from college for doing just that).

After my two years on staff, the city editor, Hal Metzger, stunned the newsroom by assigning me to a story that had the seeds to grow into one of major significance, certainly locally and possibly nationally. The prevailing thought of older reporters was that I was too young and too inexperienced. They argued one of them should have been selected.

The locale of my reporting assignment would be Newport, Kentucky, directly across the Ohio River and less than a mile from the newspaper's offices in the heart of downtown Cincinnati. It was known as Sin City, with illegal gambling rooms, nude dancers, shootouts, madams, prostitutes, crooks, grudges, citizen reformers, look-the-other-way law enforcement, heads of organized crime families, thefts, cheating card dealers, roulette wheel spinners, wealthy politicians, all-night monkey businesses, murders and occasionally missing persons never to be found.

Although the subject of my reporting was in Kentucky, I would write my stories not in the Enquirer's Kentucky office but rather at my current desk in the Enquirer's newsroom in Cincinnati, partly to keep me less likely to be compromised by the mob, which had won over other reporters.

Today, newsrooms have the noise level of libraries compared to back then, thanks to the silence brought about by computers. And now they are decimated, staffed mostly by a handful of journalism graduates wearing khakis and polos rather than crumpled shirts and slacks.

In those old days, there were only a few women reporters, and they mostly worked the softer news, except for Margaret Josten, who was treated by the editors as though she were a man. It was a rough-and-tumble newsroom, a man's place, but she won them over, even though her voice was always quite gentle.

I had not seen a major publication's newsroom until I visited while finalizing the arrangements for my hiring as a copy boy. It frightened me. How I could I concentrate on writing even one paragraph in a noisy zoo like that? The permeating odor of burning tobacco and its haze hung everywhere, with editors shouting to reporters who in turn were howling at copy boys who were running at a fevered pace in all directions.

A brief picture of the 1950s newsroom: The room blasts into action every day at 1 p.m. More than a dozen manual Royal typewriters create a clamor. Multiple phones are ringing. "Copy" was a constant yell from all directions of the room. It meant a story was ready to be quickly carried to an editor, or from the editor to the copy desk, or from the copy desk to a tube to the composing room to be set in type and placed in the paper. A tobacco spittoon was a part of each reporter's workstation as well as an ashtray, which was a foot in diameter and an inch deep. Virtually all were full at the end of the day. Reporters and editors would argue at the top of their lungs about how to approach this or that story topic.

The most important thing to the reporter was the quality of his news gathering and writing. He loved good editors, hated bad ones with passion, and exploded inside if he would be asked to write a complimentary story about one of the paper's advertisers or promote some silly interest of the publisher's wife.

The afternoon's whirring roar subsided at 7 p.m., the deadline of the first edition. The bulk of the newspaper was put together by then. That is when many of the highest-ranking editors left for the day and their lieutenant editors (I later became one) handled the stories breaking between then and 1 a.m. However, by 11 p.m., the action slowed to a trickle. That is when old-timers might throw down a shot from the stash that they kept discreetly hidden. Seldom does anything newsworthy happen on Christmas and New Year's Day. Bosses were gone and not likely to reappear. So, out into full sight came the booze. All the folks left in the newsroom hung around the copy desk (the place where they check stories and write headlines).

Those were hilarious times. It was inside talk about everything: stories about PR agents, politicians, lawyers, our entire advertising department which always was the target of our fire, judges, the Enquirer's society staff and the night-time regulars on the downtown streets. Our news competitors, newsmakers and some of our bosses were also targets of our hilarity.

My boss was Hal, the city editor who oversaw all the newsroom reporters. He was calm, cool-headed, soft-voiced, always thoughtful, insightful, accessible, helpful and caring. As you can tell, I thought the world of him. His mission was to make all of us successful. We always raised our glasses when discussing him.

Hal was a graduate of a Catholic high school, had a college degree, was a war veteran and had been a reporter for years until being promoted. He was a thin, short, wiry and athletic person and one of the few, if not the only, person in the newsroom who didn't smoke cigarettes. I never heard him swear. If he had something to say to you, he would sit on your desk, tell you why you should not do what you did, and then leave with both of you smiling.

In discussing my new assignment, Hal told me I needed to dig into the roots of the situation by sitting down with people on all sides of the story. He told me to spend time with Jack Ramey, recently retired after being a long-time Enquirer columnist and editor.

He also knew the scene: Jack gambled weekly with close friends in the back room of Newport's Flamingo Club, a restaurant that served good, reasonably priced food and drinks to the public, while in the back room the same food and drinks were free. Jack was a jolly, sensitive person with a twinkle in his eye and a smile leading to a frequent chuckle. He was about 35 years my senior, a gifted writer, and had friends everywhere, from street beggars to the top of society. He never met a person he did not like, from a crook to the crowned.

I was the new-hire copyboy at the Enquirer when my dad died young. Jack caught me sitting alone at a nearby bar not aware of the tears running down my cheeks. Jack pulled himself up onto the next stool and we chatted.

Soon, I was spilling my deepest thoughts and feelings. With never a word spoken out loud, I was afterward included in social and business conversations both in and out of the office. I was included in an unstructured group of newsmen who were the Enquirer's best journalists. It was the best gift anyone could give me at the time.

After I received the Newport assignment, Jack spent hours with me on bar stools and in the Enquirer's conference room explaining why countless Campbell County grand juries could not find vice and crime in Newport. Those grand juries always reported there was not enough evidence of lawlessness to warrant arrests. The juries usually were in session for six to eight weeks, time and time again. And they always found nothing.

This time, however, a state grand jury had been empaneled many more months than usual with jurors representing the entire state instead of just Campbell County. They met in Kentucky's capitol of Frankfort with the mission to seek and study evidence of vice and crime in Newport. Jack thought this could be pivotal. This might finally mean the breakup of a long and deep history of crime in Newport. It gave reformers hope.

Jack and Hal spent several sessions with me to help me to learn all I could about Newport crime as well as giving me names of people I should interview: several Newport lawyers, owners of Newport industries, and leaders of the Committee of 500, a reform movement of regular citizens. We agreed that sometimes I would have to go off-the-record, keeping sources secret in order to get a complete grasp of the problem. And as it later turned out, that method opened door to obtaining truthful and valuable stories.

Both Jack and Hal in separate conversations said the same thing: the key persons in cities with crime problems are prosecuting attorneys. Why? Grand juries can be their tools to support outcomes they favor.

This is important to understand:

A grand jury's sole mission is to decide if it believes there is enough evidence to arrest. It is a part of the information-gathering process to help prosecutors decide if the existing evidence is strong enough to make arrests. Nothing more. Only the prosecutor can determine if the case should go to trial.

The grand jurors are selected randomly from the rolls of citizens administered by clerks of courts. Everything that happens during grand jury hearings is secret. Not even defense lawyers are allowed in the jury rooms. The prosecutor selects witnesses to be examined by the jurors, although jurors may also ask to hear testimony from other witnesses. After grand juries learn the evidence, it is the prosecutor who interprets for the jury the law that is pertinent. Too often this process is merely a public shield for the prosecutor.

It was a long-established practice that crime bosses in Newport would halt their activities while a grand jury was in session, a necessary step to keep illicit acts from being readily apparent. It was vacation time for many in the criminal industry. Some went to the beaches, others to the mountains. Still others visited friends working their gambling and prostitution trades elsewhere.

Interestingly, they knew before anyone else when it would be safe to return to work. The roulette wheels would be spinning immediately after the jury reported. How did they know? Suspected have been the prosecuting attorneys themselves.

Would the state grand jury be any different? The crime bosses once again shut things down, so I spent my time meeting the reformers, mostly former Newport residents who had moved to the leafy, comfortable, prestigious Fort Thomas community on the hill overlooking Newport. They were angry as hell about Newport. For many, it was their native city. Interestingly, many of the organized crime leaders also lived and raised their families in Fort Thomas.

Kentucky's largest newspaper, the Louisville Courier Journal, already had a reporter on site when I received my assignment. His stories emphasized the work of the reformers. Hal wanted me to dig into both sides of the story and leave the right-or-wrong decision for our readers. Opinions, he emphasized, are for editorial pages.

During my ramp-up time, I tried several times to gain an interview with the county prosecuting attorney. He was in town but would not grant me an interview. Nor would the Police Chief or the Mayor.

I did talk with Newport business leaders. One, who owned Newport's largest dairy, told me if an underworld figure parked his car in the middle of Main Street, the police would just smile and wave while a citizen without underworld ties would be receive a citation. "There is a double standard," he said. "Those having connections to the underworld can do anything they wish. That is the worst thing about it. Hoodlums first and citizens take the hindmost."

Another told me told Newport had the most stop signs for a city of its size in the United States. There are four-way stop signs at all but a few major through streets. Those street corners "are the only places in Newport that say stop."

I was able to attend several meetings of the reformers' committee, where I met and was able to establish a confidential relationship with one of its leaders. The rapport was cemented when we discovered my fiancée and his wife were close friends. It was a stroke of luck. He continually briefed me on reformer plans. Before beginning to write stories, thanks to Jack, I also was able to sit down to with several regular patrons of the gambling establishments. I had valuable talks with sources on both sides of the story.

Whenever the state grand jury reported its findings, I would be ready.

# Chapter 2

## Mob 101

The only writing I had done up until this point was a series on West Newport and the history of how it got the way it was. The truth is, it had never been calm or peaceful.

It all began in the early 1800s, with both soldiers and river roustabouts quenching their thirsts for booze and merrymaking. Newport Barracks was established when the U. S. outpost of Fort Washington in downtown Cincinnati relocated to five acres of Newport where the Licking and Ohio rivers meet. About the same time, steamboat paddlewheels began churning on the Ohio River. Their roustabouts, after spending many months keeping boilers full of hot steam, would arrive in the Cincinnati area wanting to let loose. But Cincinnati was more heavily policed. So, the roustabouts crossed the river and made common cause with the soldiers of Newport Barracks. Those several acres became a locus for hard drinking and available women. And so Newport's well-earned reputation for vice was born.

Other factors contributed. A steel mill was built. Employees there became unionized and struck for better pay. The company hired non-union replacements, most of whom were single and from out of town. They were fiercely resented by the out-of-work union members. West Newport became a battleground between the two factions.

The Volstead Act in 1917 that brought prohibition into existence also created a huge illegal industry: production, transportation and sale of alcohol. This was true all over the country, but the thirst for booze and gambling was especially strong in Newport, Campbell County and in neighboring Kenton County. It didn't matter if you were rich or poor or what religion you were. I heard that as many as 145 betting parlors were operating within the two counties. An old-timer told me they seemed to be on every block.

George Remus, the notorious "king of bootleggers," was a lawyer and pharmacist selling from his chain of Newport drugstores legal alcohol for medical purposes, and illegal alcohol for those who wished it. He had stills hidden in basements all over the city and beyond. He was so prosperous, he purchased 10 distilleries, including Fleischmann's.

Many country residents had no problem with illegal imbibing or betting. Numerous Newport residents were on Remus' payroll. I found no evidence of federal raids.

After I established contacts with those who would be the subject of my reporting, Hal asked for stories of Newport crime. I learned about a killing six years previous in front of the Merchants Club on West Second Street. The Merchants Club was what was known as a bust-out joint, a low-level saloon with gambling, girls, and foul-mouthed drunks wanting to have their way with the waitresses and strippers. A customer walked out of the club, and the club's owner followed, shot and killed the man in the middle of the street. Newport's legal system ruled that the owner acted in self-defense.

Another time, a wealthy man was reported missing after an argument with a member of a crime family. Later, his and his wife's bodies were found shot dead in their expensive Lincoln two counties west of Newport.

I was ready to dig into these cases, but Hal said, "Don't bother. Stay in the present, unless you get a really good lead and can break the story without spending a lifetime trying."

I was sitting at my Cincinnati desk three days later, finishing a story about the Committee of 500 adding members and funding to their cause when a story began breaking in our wire room. The first bulletin was from the Enquirer's bureau in Frankfort, followed almost immediately by the Associated Press and United Press.

"Kentucky's special grand jury meeting in Frankfort for 10 months and 14 days reported this afternoon at 3 p.m. that it could find no evidence of crime or vice in the City of Newport." That story was immediately slotted for Page One, all editions.

Hal came over and told me to wait until about 7 p.m. My task: Go back to learn firsthand whether the crime bosses were back in business. Would I find evidence that the gambling halls and brothels had re-opened? "Phone as soon as you know," Hal said. "I want a paragraph on page one hopefully in time for the first edition." With heart pumping, I called a cab and was out the door.

The cab picked me up in front of the Enquirer Building.

"Where to?"

"322 West Fourth Street in Newport."

That was three blocks from where I was headed. Cabbies are inquisitive and gabby. I did not want anyone to know where I was going for fear of shattering my cover of the story I was pursuing. Then I walked three blocks to 522 York Street, where a large, bright sign shouted: Yorkshire Club.

I knew how to proceed, having been coached by Jack. There, with my head up pretending confidence, I walked past dining tables to the rear of the room, around a long counter, through a hallway that zigged and zagged into a gymnasium-sized room so brightly illuminated there wasn't ghost of a chance that a shadow could live anywhere.

I was immediately struck by the deep somber mood. No smiling. No conversing. No one seemed to be having fun. Faces were serious. Some were somber.

Jack and Hal warned me to never assume gambling was occurring. Defense attorneys can tear apart assumptions on witness stands. So, I wrote what I saw. I watched a man hand an attendant behind a booth pieces of paper that were the size and color of U.S. currency. In exchange, the attendant handed the man what looked like checker chips. I followed the man and watched him place his chips on a long table. A person was spinning a wheel at its end. He sometimes gave the man chips and other times took them away with a long stick. I then watched another man leave the table with chips, took them to the man in the booth, who in turn counted out what appeared U.S. dollars.

That was the way I described the action in my Enquirer story. After that, I sat in several witness chairs and, thanks to the counsel of Jack and Hal, it was never disputed that gambling was happening there that night at the Yorkshire.

Outside, I found a phone booth, called the Enquirer and dictated a several-paragraph story about gambling being in full swing. It missed the first edition, which already was on the streets, but it appeared on page one in the remaining four editions, including the final, which was by far the largest in circulation.

The downstate grand jurors just hours ago reported they could not find enough evidence of gambling to recommend arrests to the prosecuting attorney. That was gambling. So let's go see about vice.

I told the cab driver what I was looking for, and I used extremely impolite words. I felt the vulgar terminology would add to my cover.

He took me to what looked like an old but nice home on West Second. The street was dark, with few lights anywhere. The driver told me to go to that door and knock hard. After paying the driver, I had only 25 cents left. I hadn't planned on spending anything the rest of the day. Those were the times before credit cards or cash machines. My press pass was good for any Yellow Cab, but they were not allowed to pick up fares in Kentucky. How would I get home? I would worry about that later.

I knocked. The latch clicked. A heavy-set older woman with gray hair cracked open the door just a few inches. There was subdued light behind her.

"I'm looking for a girl."

"Take the walkway there and I will meet you at the side door."

There, I was welcomed into a kitchen. She unquestionably was the sergeant, making introductions to four women in skin-tight blouses and skirts and who appeared to be in their 30s. Each had brilliant scarlet lips, rigid smiles and eyes lacking even the tiniest measure of twinkle. It was a hot night and all the windows were wide open.

"Come on, mister," said the sergeant. "Make up your mind. Which girl do you want to take?" She was no longer pleasant, now scolding. Two fans were blowing. Neither was large enough to do the job. One was on a kitchen table and other was on the kitchen counter next to a cash register. A cash register on the kitchen counter! I knew that would be the lead into the story.

The girls were flirtatious, coy, but the madam was goading. "Come on, come on. Who are you going to select?" She looked like the type who would come after me with a rolling pin. "Make up your mind," she snarled.

"I can't. I have no money. Only 25 cents."

"What do you mean?" She was now yelling. "I don't believe that!"

The madam started toward me. One of the windows was directly behind me and we were on the ground floor. I jumped and ran.

Months later, that jump brought laughs in two courtrooms, one county and the other downstate, including both judges and everyone in the courtrooms.

I shared a small house near downtown Cincinnati with a friend, Luke Feck, who also was on the Enquirer staff. From a phone booth, I called him for a ride. After arriving home about 2 a.m., I worked on the story until 5:30 a.m., vetting each word and massaging each paragraph, tweaking and buffing. I wanted everything expressed perfectly, because I felt the story would be pivotal to the community. All of this was happening only hours after the grand jury report.

I began my story with the state jurors' inability to find vice in Newport and my trip to West Second Street where I found girls and a cash register on the kitchen counter.

Then the second paragraph was a mere three words:

Love for sale.

I knew those words would likely attract readership.

I arrived with the completed story at the Enquirer at 1 p.m.

Just before the deadline of the first edition, Hal came to me and said, "I have discussed this with the managing editor. We decided not to put your byline on this. It is too dangerous. We are looking out for your safety.

"Instead of being the usual byline of Dan Pinger, of the Enquirer staff, it will read, by an Enquirer reporter. No Dan Pinger. Further, it was decided all your future Newport stories will be handled that way. However, not a word of the story will be changed. It will not go through the normal editing process. A copy editor will only add the headline."

I smiled and said I understood, but the truth was I was crushed. I saw this story as being a bonanza to my reputation as a journalist. Now, no one would know who wrote it.

When you hold the front page of a newspaper, every reporter wants his story where your right thumb touches the paper. Some 99% of readers scan that position first. And that is where this story was positioned, and it ran two columns to the bottom of the page. You can't beat that. It also was carried by the Associated Press, first in its own shorter rewrite of the story, and then the longer version just as I wrote it. Both went "A" wire, meaning it was sent to every important Associated Press newsroom in the nation. It even appeared internationally.

As soon as they read it, my colleagues surrounded me with congratulations. The foreman from the composing room a floor below climbed the stairs to say: "Good job, kid." "Kid" is the way he addressed all Enquirer writers under age 40.

After work, my friends and I usually visited a downtown bar or two. As we entered Willie's Little Club on Walnut Street, most of the regulars already knew I was the writer and were complimentary of the story: politicians, other newsmen, business elite, expensive call girls and members of the Cincinnati vice squad.

However, I sensed displeasure in some as they smiled and shook my hand. Gambling and girls were a winning combination in luring conventions and business to the city. Convention visitors spent millions on both sides of the Ohio River.

A cab driver came to the Enquirer newsroom the next day to say my photo was being sought in Cincinnati to distribute to all taxi drivers in Northern Kentucky, with explicit instructions not to take me to any place where there was illicit activity.

Sure enough, I learned the next day it was posted in every cab. And not just me, but also the face of Al Schottelkotte, the hard-hitting head of the WCPO-TV news operation. We both were digging news from every shadow. I was pleased to be thought of as a danger to the mob along with such a respected and tough journalist.

Soon after, my car mysteriously burned in my home driveway. The Enquirer editorialized about its reporters risking their lives in Newport. Writing reporters (plural) was to protect me.

I wish they hadn't. I was a young bachelor working nights and weekends dreaming of attracting female interest.

# Chapter 3

# An Afternoon with "Sleepout Louie"

I was on time for the 3 p.m. meeting that Jack Ramey had arranged for me. Ramey had been friendly with several of the mob gambling chieftains for years. I wanted to know the underworld's side of the story. That was part of my job. Jack set up a meeting for me and assured them to these two ground rules: that they would be anonymous sources and I would never disclose their names.

"They will talk," Jack said, "if it is for background only. They cannot risk being known as the sources for the story."

And so I arrived at The Flamingo Club, at 633 Monmouth Street. In the front was a plain-Jane restaurant with only a few customers there when I arrived. Employees were cleaning up from lunch and preparing for the evening customers. Hidden from view was the casino itself, which was in the back of the building.

A short, thin, graying man in his late 50s rose from a booth and came over to greet me. He was rumpled and dressed in clothes that could have been sold at a clothing outlet. He could easily be mistaken for being a low-level clerk in the backroom of an office or a gentle, nice elderly grandad. No. In truth, he was "Sleepout Louie" Levinson, one of the kingpins of the mob who, with his brothers Ed and Mike, ushered the potent Cleveland Crime Syndicate into Northern Kentucky more than 20 years earlier.

This came about shortly after the end of prohibition hobbled bootlegging. The leader of one of the nation's five most powerful crime families, Lucky Luciano, saw the danger of the families destroying one another in their quest for new territory. So, a commission of the strongest families was established, with Luciano as its chairman, and decisions made by majority vote. This was brilliant of Luciano. Going forward, he dominated the commission.

The Cleveland Syndicate was viewed as being immensely powerful, and therefore had the support of Luciano and the commission. In Northern Kentucky, the population for years relished gambling and retained its thirst for alcohol, thanks to the soldiers and roustabouts who led the way more than 100 years previously. The Luciano commission approved the Syndicate's bid, allowing Cleveland's entry into Northern Kentucky in the early 1930s with "Sleepout," Ed and their brother Mike Levinson arriving to take charge.

In fact, "Sleepout" already had a small stake in the Greater Cincinnati area. It was he who a few years earlier delivered a large loan from the Cleveland Syndicate in order to launch the first casino in Greater Cincinnati. That was the Arrowhead Club in Branch Hill, Ohio, which appealed to the wealthy residents of nearby Indian Hill, Ohio.

One owner of the Arrowhead was Sammy Schrader, who also was a part owner of the Walk A Show at 5600 Vine Street in Elmwood Place and the Paddock Club in St. Bernard, both in communities surrounded by Cincinnati. Other part owners of those clubs included brothers Ed and Mike Levinson.

Ed had flawlessly managed several casinos first in Detroit and then Cleveland and became the Syndicate's go-to expert on casino operations before coming to Newport. Ed was called "the biggest bookmaker in Detroit," was associated with famed mobster Bugsy Siegel, and was a partner of Meyer Lansky, who was known as "the accountant" of many mob investments.

In Newport, the brothers founded the Flamingo, took over the Yorkshire, bought and later sold the Glenn Rendezvous, Beverly Hills Country Club and in neighboring Kenton County, the Lookout House.

Then after two years, Ed left Newport to open and manage casinos in Miami, then the Bahamas, Cuba and elsewhere.

Meanwhile, "Sleepout" and Mike stayed in Newport to oversee Syndicate business while operating the Flamingo. "Sleepout" also owned the Bobben Realty Company, which was the largest layoff betting bank in the nation. Layoff banks serve bookies who need help covering large bets.

That afternoon at the Flamingo Club I wanted to begin the conversation with a soft opening, hoping it would relax us both. His brother Mike had now joined us, but "Sleepout" did all the talking.

"Why are you called '"Sleepout?"' I asked, trying to get things rolling.

"I play a lot of cards. I always seem to get sleepy and take naps. When I awaken, I would rejoin the game. They always laugh."

"Do you sign your name that way?"

"No. But remember, our promise is that you will not use my name in any way in your story."

"Absolutely," I said, and I leaned across the table and we shook hands.

At the beginning of our conversation, he expressed high regard for Jack, who for years had been a regular gambler at the casino behind the restaurant. I told him Jack had always complimented him for his honest games.

I then asked about the mob leadership. His answer was deafening silence. I was not surprised. My research caused me to expect such a response. "Omerta" is the mafia's code of silence. It originated in Sicily when Spanish armies would invade the island and enslave its citizens. It became an unwritten law for citizens to deal with their own problems rather than with established governments that they did not trust to be fair. "Sleepout" lived by that law.

I asked what was foremost on their minds with the Newport shutdown. The clubs had re-opened for exactly one day after the state grand jury finished, and then closed down again. I wanted to know why.

"Hurt? It is killing us. Top casino professionals are rare. If we were to open tomorrow, next week or next month, we probably couldn't because we wouldn't have the staff of skilled, career dealers and staff. Good ones are few and far between," he said.

"They're saying now that they're all on flying to Las Vegas. They call it the Newport/Vegas special. They laugh when they board the plane and see all the others they know. And, I'll tell you another thing. I understand they all have found employment already and there is not a casino on the Strip that has not employed at least one."

Then he unloaded: "Newport has increasingly turned nasty, and it has been happening more and more over years. It is no longer safe from crime and the rubbish that goes with it. It has been causing many of our longtime customers from coming because of the riff-raff bust-outs over there and the cheating games down there," motioning in the general direction with his arms. "They have to drive through all of it to get to us."

I sat stunned at the way this important mobster was talking, tearing apart a mob. But it was not his mob.

One of the things I learned from "Sleepout" that day was that a huge divide had formed in the 1950s between the honest gambling clubs and clubs that cheated their patrons. In "Sleepout's" view, his people ran the honest clubs, and another group of people, and those associated with the Steubenville mob, ran many of the cheat joints.

"Gambling," he said, "is a recreation and is played over the world. Many people love it and look forward to their weekly or monthly trip to a casino."

"Your games are known for being honest," I said. "Jack has made a point of that."

"Yes. They always have been and always will be," he said.

"Is the Beverly Hills honest?" I asked him.

The reply was immediate. "Yes."

"Tropicana?"

Showing anger, he muttered, "That crooked bunch."

He told me, "We have been here nearly 30 years, but we cannot hold out much longer."

Many of his professional staff were already in Les Vegas, with others were packing to go. His shoulders slumped as he was talking and Mike was quiet.

"Will you move to Vegas?" I asked him.

"I don't know. I keep hoping for a turnaround. But for years now, it just keep getting worse."

I asked, "What would you do in Vegas?"

"Don't know. But I'll tell you what. The games are honest out there. It is hard to believe that everything is clean and honest out there, while we are being drowned here by a dishonest neighborhood."

Again, I asked, "What would you do out there?

"I do not know, but we have a brother out in Vegas."

At that time, I did not know that his brother Ed had ownership and management roles in many of the big-name establishments in Las Vegas. He owned 72% of the Fremont, others at a lesser percent.

"When did your gambling staff decide to leave?" I asked him.

"We were sinking for years here in Newport. So, there was much unrest. "Then we were closed all that time when the state grand jury was out. We were open for one night and closed the next day. These are smart people. That caused them to see clearly the writing was on the wall. They had no future here."

I asked him, "What are you going to do next?"

"Probably move to Vegas. All the games are honest out there."

I asked him how he personally felt about this.

"I raised my family here in Fort Thomas," he replied. "I love it here. I do not want to leave."

I thanked him for his time and candor and made my way back to the newsroom. I knew that the power of this story would be limited by the fact that I could not allow the readers know to whom I was speaking, nor could I write what he said.

I could only write that the professional gambling staff was fleeing from Newport to Les Vegas, according to an unnamed source.

Now, after 60 years, I believe enough time has passed to identify my source. But as I look back, I wonder what might have been if, at the time, I could have reported that the major mob casinos are closing their doors and leaving Newport forever.

Sure enough, two weeks later, the Flamingo closed its restaurant, never to be opened again. Certainly, there have been bits of gambling and prostitution rise here and there since then, but never to the full swing it once was.

The "Sleepout" interview gave credence to what we had been hearing that the so-called "mob" existed in many different forms, some contributing to society in their own ways.

For example, Sammy Schrader, the head of Beverly Hills Country Club for 20 years, purchased a large piece of land in Bellevue, Ky., graded it himself with his bulldozer, and built a nice baseball diamond. Then he donated it to the city for residents to enjoy. Schrader's casino was the other place singled out by "Sleepout" for having honest games. I tried, of course, to meet Sam Schrader. I wanted to do the interview at his park, but I failed in many tries.

In Newport, some of the clubs known for cheating and roughness were connected to another group of mobsters from Steubenville, while the honest games were generally associated with the Cleveland mob.

Dean Martin, the late singer, once told me about his two years living in Cincinnati and working as a dealer at the Beverly Hills Supper Club. Martin himself was from Steubenville, but he chose to work not at the Steubenville clubs but at Beverly Hills.

As a reporter, I once met the airplane carrying him and Frank Sinatra to Cincinnati. They both were like young kids looking forward to a birthday party. They were going straight to Beverly Hills, refusing to sit for an interview with me.

# Chapter 4

# George Ratterman and Tito Carinci

Shortly after the Kentucky grand jury found no evidence of vice or crime in Newport, the Committee of 500 reform group announced George Ratterman as its candidate for the Campbell County sheriff's position in the upcoming election.

The office of sheriff is the second most important crime-fighting position after that of the prosecuting attorney. Ratterman was a football hero of local and national prominence who had been in the sports headlines for years. He was a resident of the upper-middle class community of Fort Thomas along with his wife, Anne, and their eight children.

Ratterman was a part of a highly respected family. His grandfather was prominent, his father a well-respected attorney and his uncle was a revered Jesuit priest who became Dean of Men at Xavier University.

Since then I have read that Robert Kennedy, then the U.S. Attorney General, was influential in getting Ratterman into the race. I had heard rumors of this, and every Thursday for months I phoned the U.S. Attorney General's office offering what the Enquirer was learning in exchange for what they knew. The conversations became regular friendly chats. No information was ever exchanged, but I continued to phone. My contact's response was always: If we can, we will. Those conversations later proved to be golden.

Ratterman also was a lawyer, and one of his legal clients had been the American Football League before it merged with the National Football League.

He was considered among the greatest athletes in Notre Dame University history. He was the back-up quarterback to Johnny Lujack, but he also lettered in basketball, baseball and tennis. He went on to be an outstanding quarterback for the Buffalo Bills, and then the Cleveland Browns, taking over from the legendary Otto Graham. The team's owner and no-nonsense coach and team owner, Paul Brown, wasn't necessarily a fan, and described him to us at the Enquirer as an "eccentric." But Otto Graham called Ratterman the funniest guy in the NFL.

The story goes that one time a player, as usual, ran in from the sidelines with the next play Brown wanted executed. Ratterman heard it, said he did not like it, and told the player to go get another. Laughter exploded in the huddle, and several had to run and stop the messenger from returning to the sidelines.

However, two weeks after his picture appeared on the cover of Sports Illustrated, Rattermna's knee gave way, and that suddenly ended his sports career. He later became a national sports radio and TV commentator.

I first interviewed Ratterman in his large, plush office atop the Carew Tower, which at that time was the tallest building in downtown Cincinnati. It was the day after he announced his candidacy. He was tall, blond, unusually calm, cordial and very serious.

I had one main question and I asked it several different ways: "Why do you want to be the Sheriff of Campbell County?" His wife's family was deeply rooted in Newport and Fort Thomas, but he was a native of Cincinnati. In those days there were big cultural differences between Ohio and Kentucky, a divide that multiple interstate traffic bridges over the Ohio River eventually minimized and changed.

"Would you have trouble winning a Kentucky election, having been born and raised in Cincinnati? My view is many Kentuckians look at Ohioans with resentment. Could that be an obstacle to your election and at times lead to misunderstandings?" I asked.

Without hesitation, he looked at me and replied, "No."

He said he knew what he was getting into and was not worried. I waved my hand around at his spacious, paneled, deep-carpeted office, where he held a position as a big-ticket financial planner and stockbroker, and asked if he thought he would eventually have second thoughts about giving up so much.

He did not blink an eye. "There is an important job to do," he said.

Question answered!

During this time, I was fortunate to have several trusted, deep sources in the reform group, who could separate hearsay from the truth. Key to me was Ed Hengelbrok, who I knew socially. He was a principled and articulate leader of the Committee of 500 who kept me well informed of its plans and thinking. His family originally was from Newport where he was president of his family's manufacturing company. He was a founder of the Northern Kentucky Chamber of Commerce and was well-connected. In fact, his sister Anne was married to George Ratterman. They all resided in the same Fort Thomas neighborhood.

Henry Cook was another source. Henry was a talented, experienced and well-respected attorney, and his brother was one of the founders of the Committee of 500. Henry and Ed were the clearest-thinking representatives I met from the reform group. I could always reach them. They were always straightforward and never hid the facts. They gave me important information. If they couldn't tell me, they would tell me so.

By this time, the big-time casino operators had already left town or were on the way out. All that was left was the smaller Tropicana Club at the Hotel Glenn in Newport, which was a "b" or "c" player and probably it was only a matter of time before it closed. I could tell by the way "Sleepout" talked; he would have given it an "f."

Also still operating in Newport was the Sportsman's Club, which was the headquarters of the largest numbers gambling racket in the Midwest. And scattered here and there were some small gambling operations clinging for their lives in the sea of change.

Managing the Glenn Hotel and its Tropicana was Tito Carinci, a football star of Cincinnati's Xavier University where, in 1957, he was named an All-American linebacker of the smaller-university leagues. He had tryouts with the Chicago Bears and the Green Bay Packers, where he made it all the way to the final cut.

Tito Carinci had been raised in Steubenville, Ohio in a part of Ohio where low-level bust-out bars were active. It was said he was from a good family. His father was the woodworking teacher at Central Catholic High School. Criminality was not in his background nor his family's.

I wanted to learn Carinci's plans moving forward. I phoned the Glenn Hotel, spoke with him, and we arranged to have a late dinner at the old Tri-City Yacht Club, moored on the Ohio River between Newport and Bellevue. When I arrived, Carinci was already seated with two women – strippers – next to him, Juanita Hodges (her stage name was April Flowers) and Rita Desmond. Both were dressed in conservative dark dresses and minimal makeup.

Carinci told me the Tropicana no longer had gambling or prostitution. It was just a nice supper club, he said, popular with middle-class folks who could dine and dance there on their wedding anniversaries. He talked about his Xavier University heroics, his Army service as a commissioned lieutenant (as a graduate of the

University's ROTC program). He held center stage the entire evening.

He was reminiscent of a TV game show host: charming, convincing, laughing, a pleasing conversationalist, joking, persuasive, fun to be with. All the while the women said little, nor did he ever direct the conversation to them. He was believable until I began to notice, later in our discussion, that he was contradicting much of what he had said earlier about various topics in our discussions. I thought it strange.

Several weeks later, in early April of 1961. I was sitting at my desk in the Cincinnati newsroom when the Enquirer's Kentucky office phoned: the Newport police had just caught George Ratterman at the Glenn Hotel, half clothed and drunk, with stripper April Flowers.

I sat stunned for a moment, caught my breath, and reached for the phone and called Ed Hengelbrok. Hengelbrok was still getting information about his brother-in-law's arrest early that morning, and promised to call me when he learned more.

Ratterman's candidacy for sheriff was immediately in question. I gave money to a copyboy to bring me a BLT from Bob Jones' Bar. It might be a long night.

Hengelbrok phoned again shortly afterwards to say all major local press were being phoned invitations to Ratterman's home in Fort Thomas. Ed, who resided nearby, met me at the door, and introduced me to his sister, Anne Hengelbrok Ratterman.

It was a well-appointed home but not ostentatious, with large rooms, thick noise-muffling carpet, subdued colors and attractive and well-organized furniture. It had a peaceful and quiet feeling about it all.

I shook hands with George and his friend, Tom Paisley from Medina, Ohio, who was in town visiting. Both had been footballers, and stood noticeably taller than those of us with notepads, microphones and cameras. And both looked dazed, faces serious and strained. Neither could explain what had happened. It was no longer peaceful and quiet. Reporters interrupted each other asking the same question in different ways: "What in the hell were you doing?"

That has never been my style. I moved away from the contingent and went over to Tom Paisley to attempt to drill deeper. He told me he and George thought it would be a daringly provocative idea to meet with Carinci, who had been wanting to get together with George. They both knew that if Ratterman was elected sheriff, the Tropicana would be high on his list to close.

Later in court, both Ratterman and Paisley said they met with Carinci in a Cincinnati bar. Paisley then left to retire to his Cincinnati hotel room.

In talking with people who knew George well, there was a consistent description that he was a fine person with a curious mind, which sometimes led to an occasional flash of off-the-wall folly. Paul Brown thought that he could be a loose cannon. So that may explain how Ratterman got into this predicament.

# Chapter 5

# Trial of the Century (and a Lesson in Humility)

It was described by some media as "The Trial of the Century." It had sex, fame, crime, intrigue, straight-laced citizens organizing against the mob, and a possible frame-up, all in the small Kentucky town that had become known across the nation as Sin City.

It was 3 o'clock in the morning on May 9, 1961, when Ratterman, based on an anonymous tip, was arrested at the Glenn Hotel on charges related to prostitution. The trial would be a week later. We at the Enquirer assumed newspapers and magazines from across the country would be there because of the trial's sensational nature. And we were correct.

Covering the story with me would be the Enquirer's first woman general assignment reporter, Margaret (Maggie) Josten. I would be reporting the straight news of the day, and she would write feature articles, such as a more in-depth interview with someone related to the trial. We were the paper's team, whose work each day would be read by hundreds of thousands of people.

But I was worried. I had never covered any trial in my life. I was afraid of failing.

I remembered what had happened to Bill Collins when I was a copyboy. He was the best reporter on the staff, a star among several stars. All his stories were the products of solid research, smart structure and clear and interesting writing. When depth of its subject was required, he dug down into the sub-basement. He had sensitivity as both a writer and a person.

Bill wrote a brilliant five-part series, all appearing on page one of the paper, all editions, about the migrants to Cincinnati from the mountains of Kentucky, West Virginia and Tennessee, and particularly the availability of services to help them adjust to life in the city. It was a major issue locally at that time. He sat down with university professors, social workers, medical professionals, employment specialists, housing officials and politicians to better inform our readers what was being done, what needed to happen, and how the problem could be solved.

At that time, only four relatively old, two-lane bridges crossed the Ohio River at Cincinnati. Three of the bridges were exceptionally narrow. It was a sore point for both Kentuckians and Ohioans not to be able to easily travel across state lines. Therefore, the differences between the two were pronounced.

So, when one of Bill's interview subjects was asked what immediately should be done to ease the problem, his answer, most unfortunately, was, "Burn the bridges." By this, he meant to halt the flow of people from the south until the region strengthened its delivery social services for the migrants.

That quote appeared in the first paragraph of the series, meant to reflect the radical thinking to address a social system overwhelmed. Instead, many readers interpreted "burn the bridges" to mean that the Enquirer, and the speaker, were saying that Ohio should keep out people from the south, that Ohioans were superior to Kentuckians, West Virginians and Tennesseans. Thousands canceled their Enquirer subscriptions in protest, many using not nice language.

Bill was no patsy. He was a Korean War veteran. But for weeks, maybe months, you could see the pain in his face, and he became more withdrawn. Most reporters I knew were sensitive people.

That series had to pass the inspection of the managing editor at some point along way. All major stories do. It had to have been read and approved by the city editor, then by the person sitting in a slot in the center of a round table, who gave it a quick look before handing it to one of his copy editors sitting of the rim of the table, who would have checked every word and punctuation mark, correcting problems and composing its headline, then back the slot man for a final brief look at it, and then to the composing room to be set in hot type.

It is a shame not one of those realized that the words "burn the bridges" could have an unintended implication. It may have been little, or no, problem if the article was not on page one, which is scrutinized more carefully by the readers.

My stories about the Newport mob would certainly be in that position, and I would have to work hard to get the stories straight, while also being sensitive to any way their meaning might be mistaken.

Then I made matters even tougher on myself. Amidst criticism from some traditionalists, I occasionally had tried out the writing style of the New York tabloids to get the across a story clearly in just a few words and sentences. It is far more difficult because each word must fit perfectly with the one before and after it. forming a clear stream of the story. When it happens, you win. But when the words are not, you have a mess on your hands.

I had used that style several times in my news writing and Hal gave me the green light to use it if I wished on some trial stories. That abrupt tabloid style of writing had become an issue of ridicule by an older, cranky combat veteran named Ed S. Ed was a good medical and science reporter, but had a generally angry personality. For some unknown reason, he particularly targeted me from the time I was a copyboy, saying in a loud, authoritative voice: "You will never make it here. You cannot write. I'm just telling you this for your own good."

My reaction was pure hate. To show what kind of person he was, he was the reason the newsroom no longer had company-hosted Christmas parties. At the last one, he called the managing editor a "fat old fart" to his face. However, I must admit, Ed could write about science succinctly and powerfully.

In mentally preparing for the trial, I faced the reality that I had no experience in covering a trial, and that type of reporting was far from my strength. I am not a shouting-questions type of reporter. Bob Firestone, one of my editors, would shout across the newsroom with a twinkle in his eye: "There's hard-nose, hard-assed Dan Pinger." Many times, after an interview, the interviewee would say they had not expected someone so mild to be such a hard news reporter.

But that style worked for me. I had been lucky in uncovering unreported news, often in a quiet sit-down chat with an interviewee who dropped his or her guard.

One time, the Teamsters' Union leader, Jimmy Hoffa, was in the city concerning an explosive matter and, in a relaxed manner after Hoffa spoke, I learned from his right-hand man some key information about the union's plans. That information was published at the top of our page one and then carried by wire services across the nation. Sometimes, I found a better story after a press conference in a phoning the interviewee afterwards. My opening would typically be something like, "I want to make certain I understood what you said..."

Facing the coverage of a trial, I hated the thought of having to focus strictly what was said in the courtroom. I would have loved to have traded jobs with Maggie.

The trial was held in sweltering early May heat, with no air conditioning, in the more than century-old Newport City Building, constructed of red brick with stone trimmings and a bell tower in its center with two high, pointed roof towers at each end. It is a relic of history.

The jury box was reserved for the press. In those days, newspapers were where most of the public received their daily news. Two front-row seats in the middle were reserved for Maggie and me. Since the Enquirer had the largest circulation, Maggie and I were like a queen and king. The room was packed with media. Most were from New York, others from across the nation. Many members on the nationwide press wanted to attach themselves to Maggie and me to get background information about the case and its set of characters. We politely obliged, but only with information already in the public domain, nothing further. What we knew and they didn't we considered the sole property of the Enquirer.

This also was the first time I would be teaming with a colleague working the same story from the same location but with different responsibilities. She was there to conduct interviews and I was there focus on the trial itself, and both of us were keeping the lines open for new information.

The proceedings were conducted by a municipal judge. Ratterman's defense was directed by Henry Cook, of the Committee of 500, and the prosecution by Charles Lester, who began his presentation of the case.

The proceedings moved slowly. Carinci testified Ratterman knew what he was doing and got caught in the act. In cross examination, Carinci denied it was a set-up. At each recess, Ed Hengelbrok walked over to ask me to please hold judgment. I told him I could not think about winning or losing but only the facts learned each day. Tito Carinci walked over to say the truth is coming out. He kept saying Ratterman got caught and was too weak to admit it.

When April Flowers and Rita Desmond, another Newport stripper, took the stand, both said they knew nothing about a frame-up and Ratterman had had a few drinks and was in a happy mood.

As the days of the trial unfolded, I wrote two stories in my new, blunt, tabloid style of writing. The evening prior to the trial's last day, Maggie and I, as usual, finished our stories and then proceeded to dinner at the newsroom's favorite restaurant, The Cricket, in downtown Cincinnati. There we ran into our friend, Mike Maloney, who had left the Enquirer's political beat to enter politics, eventually becoming an Ohio state senator. The three of us discussed the trial and Mike suggested we pay Carinci a visit. We might learn something newsworthy, he said, and Maggie and I agreed.

The two of us went over to the Tropicana, walked inside, and I asked for Carinci, I gave Maggie's name and mine. He was with us in a flash, led us to his private table and moments later April Flowers appeared, dressed in a conservative black dress. Everything about her was subdued. This surprised me after seeing how the prostitutes dressed at the whorehouse. If I did not know and had to guess, I would have said she was a successful junior executive.

Carinci was his usual game-show self. He laughed at how sex-hungry Ratterman must have been to get caught. Carinci kept saying Ratterman knew full well what he was doing and now he was blaming Tito.

The only time I saw April smile was when she danced on the stage. No raunchy moves, just smoothly gliding around. Not flirtatious but yes, titillating. The question was how and why a 26-year-old beauty queen ever got caught up in all of this?

Back in court the next morning, Lester, in making his case, mentioned the word "photography." Ratterman's attorney Cook immediately erupted, shouting that this misdemeanor case had been going along too long, day after day, dragging his client's good reputation through the mud.

"We will show the court we know a bit about photography,'" shouted Cook.

The judge asked the prosecutor how much longer he would need. Lester said he was about to finish and he did so quickly. The proceedings were adjourned for a lunch break. And Lester was never seen at the trial again.

At the end of his testimony, Carinci said he visited his priest that morning and swore his testimony was true. Then he turned to Ratterman and asked, "George, can you do that?"

The afternoon session opened with an assistant in Lester's place guiding the defense team. Maggie and I wondered what could have possibly happened to Lester. The nation was focused on this trial, and the prosecutor had disappeared with no notice?

Cook's first witness was a large, purposeful grandma figure. You just knew the mob and the prosecution better not get between her and her God.

"Yes," she was Christian. "Yes," she never missed church on Sundays and Wednesday evenings. "No," she never lied. "Yes," she made her home with her daughter and son-in-law. "Yes," the phone rang about every three minutes beginning about 2:30 the morning of the raid. "Yes," her son-in-law made his living as a photographer.

Maggie and I leaned together and whispered, "That's the ball game and that must be why Lester disappeared at Cook's mention of 'photography'."

Her daughter then took the stand and collaborated her mother's testimony.

Then the daughter's husband, Thomas Withrow, testified that he had met with an attorney two weeks before the night in question, who said Withrow would be well compensated if he would take a photograph at the Glenn Hotel at 2:30 a.m. the same morning the police arrested Ratterman there.

The more he thought about it, the more Withrow grew convinced that his photo was designed to frame someone, and the more he discussed the situation with his wife and his mother-in-law, the three of them agreed it was business he would not accept.

Without a photograph of Ratterman and Flowers in bed to blackmail Ratterman, the plan fell apart, said Cook. Then the fallback was to have the Newport police conduct the raid and photograph a partly undressed and drugged Ratterman.

Then another piece of evidence emerged: As soon as Ratterman arrived home after the raid at the Glenn Hotel, his wife, Anne, insisted on an immediate medical examination by their family physician. Three times the normal dose of chloral hydrate, or knockout drops, was found in Ratterman's blood.

At this sudden turn, the acting prosecutor moved to have the case dismissed. The judge pounded his gavel and the trial was over in a matter of seconds.

Ed Hengelbrok immediately came across the room, said nothing, but his face was flushed. I stood and shook his hand and we each went our own way.

I later asked Hengelbrok how they learned about the photographer. He said the Withrows were members of a church that was the hotbed of the reform push. Its pastor was Cook's brother.

Maggie and I rushed back to the office to file our story. I struggled with the new writing style, but I thought my story had turned out fine. But Hal read it and did not like it. He said the new writing style wasn't working and that it needed to be rewritten.

"Fine, give it back to me," I said.

"No, go home and rest. It has been a big week for you."

"I'll rewrite it straight," I told him.

"No, no," said Hal. "Get out of here and get some sleep."

Hal took my story and notes and gave them to another reporter. I felt angry and ashamed, which was deepened when I saw that the rewriter was Ed S., of all people.

I read and reread the story in the paper the next morning, Ed working from my notes. I sat in thought as I read his words.

Yes, Hal had been correct in taking the story from me. The way I had written it was clearly not as effective as the way Ed had handled it.

# Chapter 6

# I Thought My Work Was Done, and Then ...

Ratterman was easily elected sheriff. He immediately fired some deputies and began successful raids.

One sizable illegal operation remained: The Sportsman's Club at 333 Central Avenue. It was owned by Frank "Screw" Andrews (nee Andriola) who had been raised in Cincinnati's Little Italy, in the Walnut Hills neighborhood west of Gilbert Avenue and south of McMillan Avenue. It was in the streets of Little Italy where "Screw" Andrews learned and practiced the numbers game, originally known as the Italian Lottery.

Here's how it works: The bettor gambles that his selection of three digits will win a random draw the next day. For example, the game operators might predetermine that the play would be on the third, fourth and fifth numbers of the total shares traded at the New York Stock Exchange, and the number of shares traded were 35,363,247, then the winning numbers would be 363.

Often, the daily handle at a racetrack was used as the numbers source. Bets could be made for as little as $1 and the payoff could be as high as $500. The game was played mostly among poor and working-class individuals.

Which means these players were not typical Enquirer readers. Most of our readership was in suburbia, and the editors were extremely mindful that too much vice and crime would be distasteful to them, especially during the breakfast hour.

I researched and wrote a five-part series about local prostitution after informative interviews with law enforcement, religious leaders, prostitutes and their regular customers. It was judged fit to print by Hal and the managing editor but killed by the publisher. The publisher believed the Enquirer had done enough coverage of Newport's sore thumb and it was time to cease publishing its cringe-worthy news in all editions. Future reporting would be handled by

Kentucky Bureau reporters for the Kentucky edition only. So, my Newport vice and crime mission was halted – mostly.

I kept my hand in, just a little bit. The Kentucky Bureau had a staff of reporters covering their beats. The Bureau chief made assignments, read their work and sent the stories to the Kentucky Editor in Cincinnati. The Kentucky Editor worked five days of a six-day operation. So, when I returned from my Newport assignment, I filled in for him one day a week and during his vacations and sick days.

I had a similar assignment to substitute as editor of the Ohio edition one night a week, and as the Cincinnati final edition editor on Saturdays for Sunday's paper. That left me one day a week to handle other assignments, write features, comb Greater Cincinnati for good stories, and edit the Youth page that ran each Saturday.

My housemate, Luke Feck, and I shared a large two-bedroom house next to Eden Park on a hilltop overlooking downtown Cincinnati. We also were the young, college-educated guys who, at the end of most workdays, had to go down one floor to the composing room to supervise the makeup of the paper.

The composing room was too hot for air conditioning because of the melting lead in the Linotype machines used for hot metal typesetting. It took years of experience and some luck for stories to measure the proper depth you planned in the layout map you provided the press room.

A printer can put a lead pieces between lines of lead type if the story is too short. But that might not look good. However, if the stories were too long, they would need to be trimmed.

That is where Luke and I had a problem. We were young kids as far as the much older unionized tradesmen were concerned, and some of them believed we thought we were better than them. And they could make us look bad as we "supervised" the work, partially the trimming or rearranging which had to be all upside down for the printing process. Luke had responsibility for putting together various TV and entertainment pages and I had various news and feature pages to make sensible.

So, several years before my Newport assignment, Luke and I hatched a plan. We would throw a party only for the printers. We bought plenty of beer and five-gallon cans of potato chips and pretzels and invited them all to our house beginning at 10 p.m. on a Saturday. We had warned the neighbors who were mostly old and asked for their understanding. In our planning, Luke and I agreed we were not ever going to ask anyone to leave. That would go against the spirit we were trying to create

All went surprisingly well. We replaced beer and chips as needed. The party continued well into daylight Sunday, continued all day, and the last few left midmornings on Monday. They were coming and going for about 34 hours.

This party was the best investment we made in our newspaper careers. All our pages got special treatment. They made us look brilliant. Our work life suddenly got easier.

I tell you this because one night at 11:20 I was in the composing room when I got a call from the newsroom. There was a call waiting for me from the Justice Department, and they would not leave a message and they stressed it was important.

This happened just when the make-up of the pages was full of problems. I quickly looked over at the two printers. "We've got you," one of them said. That was the spirit we had been getting from the printers since the house party.

It was the friendly man on the phone, the one I had been speaking with almost weekly and getting nothing.

"Dan, this is George. I told you we were happy with what the Enquirer has been doing. Grab a photographer and be at 333 Central Ave. in Newport at midnight. Do not arrive a minute before or after. We have an agent on the door who has been there for six months just for this moment. His only mission is to be at the door to allow our agents entrance as well as to you and your photographer. No one else will be admitted."

I hung up and yelled across the newsroom at photographer Jerry Cornelius as he was leaving for the night. Enquirer photographers got nearby paid parking privileges. We both ran out to his car and were on the road to Newport in eight minutes. We arrived 10 minutes early, parked in the dark, and started a slow stroll at 11:55. We arrived on the stroke of midnight. There was a hubbub at the door. I squeezed through the crowd and reached a man blocking the entrance who was keeping everyone out. I gave him my name and motioned at Jerry who was carrying his camera and supplies. We were waved inside.

The agent-in-charge introduced himself. He said they had recruited agents from different districts around the country, but not the district covering Newport. They had all been together in Chicago for six months training for this raid. They knew what to look for from their studies of the building and all its contents. He left me to talk to one of his agents. Meanwhile, Jerry was photographing the action.

"Screw" Andrews himself was not there. Agents were raiding his home in nearby Cold Spring, Ky., by smashing down his door, taking both him and many of his records into custody. His nephew, Danny Andrews Jr., who was known as "Screw Junior," was the Sportsman's Club's manager. His hands and feet were in shackles and lashed behind his back to the bar.

This was long before cell phones, and I desperately needed to call the office to give information for page one in the Final Edition. So I asked Screw Jr. if I could make a call on the phone behind the bar. He nodded yes. After the call, I sat on the stool next to Screw Jr., just sat there for a while and then asked him for his thoughts about what was happening. He was quiet and would not look at me.

I went over to an agent who was pressing his hands at various places along the wall that covered the length of the room.

"I believe it is somewhere around here," he said as he moved his hand inches in all directions. Suddenly, the wall rolled open, exposing about 25 slot machines.

Jerry photographed agents examining elaborate communications equipment hidden in the ceiling. Obviously, that is how they kept in touch with their wide range of bookmakers. In the meantime, my mouth was parched. I took a dollar from my wallet and asked Screw Jr. would it be all right with him if I left a dollar on the cash register and reached into the cooler for a cold Coke.

"Hell no," he shouted at the top of his lungs. "Drinks are on the house."

"Hey! You over there, drinks are in the house for everyone," he kept yelling as he squirmed in his handcuffs. I placed the dollar on the cash register and grabbed a Coke. Jerry and I left about 4 a.m. and the agents were still going strong. Every one of them – each had a mission.

I wrote my story for the top right of page one (back to the traditional style of writing) and a short blurb for each of the five pages inside the paper that had been cleared of advertising to make space for this story, as well as captions for each of the maybe 29 pictures. The Enquirer's publisher had been involved in opening so much space in the paper for the story because it was an expensive action to take. Jerry had done one hell of a good job capturing the night's action. His pictures were distributed by wire services across the nation.

And that was my last Newport story. Once you fly like that, it was difficult to come back to the ground to cover the routine.

# Epilogue

## Here is What Happened to ...

**APRIL FLOWERS** phoned WCPO-TV in Cincinnati four months after the trial concluded and recanted her testimony that George Ratterman was only partially clothed when he was with her. That was untrue, she said. He was fully clothed but was unconscious, and police took him away to another room. I tracked her down by phone about 10 months later. She was living on a farm in Tennessee, had married, and was a stepmother to her husband's four children. She was exceptionally happy with her new life and wanted nothing more than to be a good wife and mother, she said. She had always seemed terribly uncomfortable the two times I was with her in Newport, looking troubled and wanting to flee.

**'SLEEPOUT LOUIE' LEVINSON** died in 1971 at age 76 at his home in Miami, Florida, where he and his brothers had businesses.

**GEORGE RATTERMAN** died in 2007 of complications of Alzheimer's at the age of 80 at his home in Centennial, Colorado, which is part of the Denver metro area. He had worked as a financial advisor and stockbroker. His survivors at the time included his wife Anne and their nine children and 23 grandchildren.

**PETER 'TITO' CARINCI** died in 2006 at age 77. He had served prison time of three years for income tax evasion and mail fraud and another five for selling heroin worth $3 million. He subsequently moved to Hermosa Beach, California, and became the manager of the Pitcher House bar on Hermosa Avenue. His survivors included his wife, Barbara, three step children and three step grandchildren.

**FRANK 'SCREW' (Andriello) ANDREWS** died in 1972 at the age of 62, found dead on a lower roof of Saint Luke Hospital in Fort Thomas where he was a patient. Two unidentified men had told a nurse they wanted to be alone with him. Then they left quickly. The window of his hospital room was broken, and Andrews' body was found on the roof two floors below. Andrews had previously served two prison terms totaling 10 years. One sentence was for five years for tax charges, while the other for five years was for gambling-related charges.

# How They Became Mobsters

In preparing for this assignment, I discovered many of today's mobsters have these traits in common: their parents arrived in the United States between 1895 and 1910 as unskilled workers from Southern Italy, Sicily, Eastern Europe and Western Russia. Their children were infants or born shortly after they arrived. Thousands of families were at that time immigrating into the United States each day through Ellis Island. They settled in the poorest of slums with virtually no possessions, hoping to escape the poverty of their own country, where they had no chance for a sound economic future. In America, it was possible.

The newly arriving fathers scraped for any work they could get. The sons at a very early age were employed as errand boys for small businesses. This led some to running bets on horses and numbers. Soon they were successful bookmakers themselves and eventually joining forces with other bookmakers to become a mob. Some used force to get their way. Others were persuasive by using non-violent harassment.

For example, the Cleveland Syndicate owned the exceptionally successful Beverly Hills Country Club in Campbell County and badly wanted to purchase the popular Lookout House in neighboring Kenton County. Both were posh, tony, deep-carpeted clubs. The Syndicate thought its several offers were fair. The last one included cash plus 40% ownership of the more lucrative Beverly Hills. The Lookout owner still said "no." So, the Syndicate each evening sent several of its members over to urinate in the Lookout House's elegantly carpeted lobby. The sale was completed quickly.

There seemed to be a fraternity of mobsters, such as the Levinsons, who did business that way. Their only crime was illegal gambling. Most of them were never convicted of a crime and were proud of that. They looked with outrage at those that did, as "Sleepout" made clear to me.

# "The Fix"

The biggest problem in Newport was not the illegal gambling, prostitution or even the bust-out joints. It was the payoffs to politicians and police to look the other way, putting gangster priorities ahead of services designed to benefit the general public.

# Many Wanted Newport to Stay the Same

Surprisingly, many residents told me they resented the reform movement and were not bothered by Newport's casinos and joints it because "it only occurs over there," as they motioned toward the general direction of downtown Newport. Their families have resided in the area for generations. For many of them, their personal financial stability depended upon jobs related directly or indirectly to the businesses the reformers wanted shuttered.

# What Was the Public's Will?

After talking to people on both sides, the will of the citizens was uncertain. However, even "Sleepout" admitted the city of Newport increasingly had become rotten. So, without honest reform, a vote of the citizens probably would have been fixed in the hoodlums' favor.

# Could Mediation Have Been the Answer?

I believe if George Ratterman, Ed Hengelbrok, "Sleepout" Louie and maybe his brother, Ed Levinson, had been able to sit together in a room with a fair mediator, Newport could have become a safe, honest community, and it would not have suffered years of job loss and depression that persisted for decades, until at last urban renewal, upscale restaurants, and family entertainment finally revitalized it.

I trusted Jack Ramey's judgment about "Sleepout," and I read everything I could get my hands on about his brother, Ed. Neither had ever been in serious trouble. His two-hour discussion with me was straight. Ed seemed the same. Hengelbrok and Ratterman would have been my selection to represent the reformers. I had straightforward discussions with three of the four. I believe a compromise could have been reached. Both sides could have won if the outcome had gone something like this: closely regulated gambling, no bust-outs, no prostitution, mild and artful strip shows, plus independent inspections to keep city services honest. I know "Sleepout" would have gone for such a compromise because we talked about it. "Sleepout" had worked hand in hand with his brother and both were highly respected among the mobs.

# The Numbers Game

The rich get their thrills from participation in gambling recreation at casinos. The average player seeks excitement at the blackjack tables. And the down-and-out find hope of winning $500 for only a $1 slot machine bet. These numbers games are huge income producers for the racketeers and are being weeded out by governments thinking that, in the long run, they are helping the poor. States own lotteries. Corporations own casinos. But who needs hope and joy and recreation the most? The poor.

A national lottery would give people who have little to dream about a chance to be electrifyingly exhilarating. Bets could be limited to prevent overspending and that could be policed by computers. It would be sharing the game of chance with those who most need a lift of their spirit.

# Mistakes Were Made

My assignment came with challenges and mistakes, most notably the time when my misstep got the *Enquirer* named in an ugly headline across the top of the front page of our major competitor, Scripps-Howard's *Cincinnati Post*. I was named in the sub-headline and story.

I had heard that the proof of the mob owning Beverly Hills Country Club could be found in its real estate deed filed at the Campbell County Court. I had attended a year of law school and was confident I could correctly interpret this deed without the assistance of an attorney. Struck gold, I thought.

My story about this deed and its connection to the mob was published the next day on the Enquirer's front page. The *Post* sent its attorney to check out the deed, and what I had reported was completely wrong. I had misinterpreted the record. I dreaded going to work the next day but, surprisingly, I did not hear one word about it. Finally, I went into Hal's office to apologize. All he said was, "Now you know what not to do the next time." He also said it was his mistake not to insist on having an attorney review the deed and my reporting.

# With Respect and Heartfelt Thanks

The story that had the most impact was the one describing vice and crime hours after the state grand jury report that found none. According to "Sleepout," that is when his talented gambling staff and ones from other Newport casinos began permanent moves to Las Vegas. They decided gambling would never be allowed to return in Newport. This story would not have been written if Hal had not told me to go over there if see if the casinos had re-opened. The true hero responsible in nailing the coffin closed was Hal.

I did not see any other media outlet get an honest interview with any top mobster leader. That door would have never opened for me if it were not for Jack Ramey, another hero.

WCPO-TV's reporting was excellent throughout the trial. A clear indication of this was when four months later April Flowers phoned the station to recant her trial testimony saying clearly Ratterman was framed by Carinci. It was the final nail pounded into Carinci's coffin, making her and the TV station co-heroes.

# Finally

I never could thank Jack and Hal enough. It was Hal who gave me so many opportunities to grow as a newsman and as a person. It was Jack who gave me savvy background and gave me free use of his extensive number of important friends.

All of that was more than 60 years ago. On any day since then, I would have dropped everything and run through fire for either of Hal or Jack. This book is dedicated to both of them, both with smart brains and kind souls. May they rest in peace while I am still here trying to make them proud.

# Known Illegal Casinos in Kentucky, 1920-1968 [1]

| Casino | City | Years of Operation | Proprietor(s) |
|---|---|---|---|
| 222 Club | Covington | 1940s-1952 | Melvin Clark and Steve Payne |
| 316 Club | Newport | 1940s-1955 | Taylor Farley |
| 345 Club | Newport | 1930s-1950s | The Bridewells |
| 633 Club | Newport | 1930s-1961 | Arthur Dennert/ Levinson Brothers |
| Alibi Club | Newport | 1940s-1955 | Melvin Clark/ Screw Andrews |
| Avenue Club | Newport | 1930s-1961 | Unknown |
| Beacon Inn | Wilder | 1930s-1940s | Buck Brady |
| Belmont Club | Newport | 1940s-1954 | Unknown |
| Beverly Hills Country Club | Southgate | 1930s-1962 | Pete Schmidt/ Cleveland Four |
| Bluegrass Inn | Newport | 1940s-1961 | Unknown |

| | | | |
|---|---|---|---|
| Club 314 | Newport | 1940s-1960s | Unknown |
| Club Alexandria | Southgate | 1940s-1961 | Unknown |
| Club Keeneland | Covington | 1940s-1952 | Unknown |
| Club Kenton | Covington | 1940s-1952 | Unknown |
| Coconut Grove | Newport | 1954-1961 | Melvin Clark/ Screw Andrews |
| Congo Club | Newport | 1950s-1961 | Melvin Clark and Steve Payne |
| Copa Club | Newport | 1940s-1961 | Melvin Clark and Steve Payne |
| Dogpatch | Covington | 1940s-1952 | Unknown |
| Flamingo Club | Newport | 1930s-1961 | Art Dennert/Levinson Brothers |
| Glenn Hotel | Newport | 1940s-1960 | Pete Schmidt |
| Glenn Rendezvous | Newport | 1940s-1960 | Pete Schmidt/ Levinson Brothers |
| Golden Horseshoe | Wilder | 1920s-1930s | Unknown |
| Grandview Gardens | Wilder | 1940s | Unknown |
| Guys and Dolls | Cold Springs | 1940s | Unknown |

| | | | |
|---|---|---|---|
| Hi-De-Ho Club | Wilder | 1940s-1955 | James Harris |
| Iroquois Club | Lexington | 1940s-1960s | Unknown |
| Kentucky Club | Covington | 1940s | Unknown |
| Kid Able Club | Newport | 1940s-1956 | The Bridewells |
| Latin Quarter | Wilder | 1947-1961 | Cleveland Four |
| Lookout House | Covington | 1930s-1952 | Jimmy Brink/ Cleveland Four |
| Mecca Club | Newport | 1940s-1950s | The Bridewells |
| Melbourne Country Club | Melbourne | 1940s-1950s | Cleveland Four |
| Merchants Club | Newport | 1940s-1961 | Cleveland Four |
| Monmouth Cigar | Newport | 1956-1961 | Unknown |
| New Concept I | Louisville | 1940s-1952 | Unknown |
| New Sportsman's Club | Newport | 1961-1968 | Screw Andrews |
| Nineteen Hole | Newport | 1940s-1950s | James Harris |

| | | | |
|---|---|---|---|
| Old Sportsman's Club | Newport | 1940s-1960 | Screw Andrews |
| Playtorium | Newport | 1951-1955 | Pete and Glenn Schmidt |
| Primrose Club | Wilder | 1940s-1947 | Buck Brady/Cleveland Four |
| Rocket Club | Newport | 1940s | Melvin Clark and Steve Payne |
| Silver Slipper | Newport | 1952-1956 | James Harris/ Cleveland Four |
| Snax Bar | Newport | 1955-1961 | Glenn Schmidt |
| Sportsman's Club | Newport | 1940s-1961 | Steve Payne/Screw Andrews |
| Spotted Calf | Newport | 1950s-1961 | Unknown |
| Stardust | Newport | 1956-1961 | Unknown |
| Stork Club | Newport | 1940s-1952 | James Harris |
| Sycamore Club | Louisville | 1930s-1960s | Unknown |
| Teddy Bear Lounge | Covington | 1940s-1952 | Unknown |
| Tin Shack | Covington | 1940s-1952 | Unknown |
| Tropicana | Newport | 1960-1961 | Cleveland Four/ Tito Carinci |
| Turf Club | Covington | 1940s-1952 | Unknown |

| | | | |
|---|---|---|---|
| Varga Club | Newport | 1940s | Melvin Clark and Steve Payne |
| Yorkshire Club | Newport | 1940s-1961 | The Bermans/ Cleveland Four |

# Known Prostitution Outlets in Newport, Kentucky, Circa 1959 [2]

| Brothel | Address | Description |
|---|---|---|
| 345 Club | 345 Central Avenue | Night House, with gambling |
| Columbia Café | 101 West Fourth Street | Night House, with gambling |
| Florence's | 212 Columbia Street | Day House |
| Fourth Street Grill | Fourth and Columbia | Night House, with gambling |
| Frolics | Monmouth Street | Bar Girls, with gambling |
| Galaxie | Monmouth Street | Bar Girls, with gambling |
| Goldy's | 28 West Second Street | Day House |
| Harbor Bar | 201 Columbia Street | Night House, with gambling |
| Kitty's | 30 West Second Street | Day House |
| Mabel's | 26 West Second Street | Day House |
| Ray's Café | 116 West Fourth Street | Brothel, open day and night |

| | | |
|---|---|---|
| Silver Slipper | Monmouth Street | Bar Girls, with gambling |
| Stardust | Monmouth Street | Bar Girls, with gambling |
| Stork Club | Monmouth Street | Bar Girls, with gambling |
| Vivian's | 21 West Third Street | Night House |
| Wanda's | 213 York Street | Day House |

[1,2] Sin City Revisited: A Case Study of the Official Sanctioning of Organized Crime in an "Open City," by Matthew DeMichele and Gary Potter, Justice and Police Studies, Eastern Kentucky University; and from J. Laudeman, *Newport, The Real Sin City*; Messick, *Razzle Dazzle*; Messick, *Letter to Mr. Pope*; Messick, *Syndicate Wife*.

# About the Author

Dan Pinger has played many roles in his long and eventful life. He raises horses. He served in the U.S. Army. He was a notably indifferent law school student and a passionate journalist. He also spent some time in academia, working as an administrator at the University of Cincinnati. He founded the Dan Pinger Public Relations agency where he and the hundreds of "Pingerites" who worked with him offered communications counsel to clients across Cincinnati and the nation for more than 25 years. And of course, Dan is a father, a son, a husband, living through all the joy and heartbreak those roles bring.

Now in his late 80s, Dan has turned his creative energy to writing. He published his first book of poetry, *Love, Laughter, Life and the Hereafter*, in 2016 and his second book, *The Ripley Ridge Storyteller*, in 2017. His third compilation of poems, *The Ripley Ridge Raconteur*, was completed in 2018. His novel *Black Smoke and Blind Men*, published in 2019, addresses global warming in a futuristic setting. *A Reporter's Memoir: When the Mob Ruled Newport* is based on Dan's time working as a newspaper reporter covering the wild and wooly days when the Syndicate thrived in Newport, Kentucky.

.

Made in the USA
Coppell, TX
20 October 2020